A GOLDEN SOUVENIR OF
RAJASTHAN

A GOLDEN SOUVENIR OF RAJASTHAN

Photography by Anthony Cassidy
Text by Tripti Pandey

UBSPD
UBS Publishers' Distributors Ltd.

First published in 1989 by UBS Publishers' Distributors Ltd., 5 Ansari Road, New Delhi-110 002, and the Guidebook Company Limited, The Penthouse, 20 Hollywood Road, Central, Hong Kong.

Title spread
Sited along the Amber road out of Jaipur, the 18th-century Jal Mahal was built by Jai Singh II as a summer retreat in the middle of Lake Man Sagar. The four walls enclosed a central garden, now an abandoned wilderness.

Right
A composite wall painting of the Bundi school showing aspects of the Krishna legend. Gopis (cowmaids), charmed by Krishna's skilful flute playing and his reputation as the Divine Lover, draw near to him and dance. Another legend has Krishna holding the Govardhan Hill aloft, supported with one finger, to protect the villages from torrential rain sent by the god Indra in his fury.

Pages 6-7
Country women dressed in colourful cloths, woven, dyed and embroidered by themselves, have come into town to take part in one of Rajasthan's great fairs. Low literacy rates among women are linked to the persistence of customs such as child marriage and sati, *a wife's self-immolation at her husband's funeral.*

Pages 8-9
The city of Udaipur reaches Lake Pichola. In the early 19th century, the famed Colonel James Tod accompanied the Maharana of Mewar to watch the Gangaur festival at Gangaur Ghat, below the Bagore haveli. The haveli is now a folklore museum run as part of the western zone's cultural centre based at Udaipur.

Pages 10-11
The local craftsmen work the yellow sandstone magnificently, carving fine screens and balconies in the buildings of the desert town of Jaisalmer.

Text by Tripti Pandey
Captions by Tripti Pandey and Toby Sinclair
Photography by Anthony Cassidy
Illustration by Mohan Lal Soni

Designed by Joan Law Design & Photography
Colour separations by Rainbow Graphic Arts Co., Ltd.
Printed in Hong Kong

ISBN: 962-217-087-0

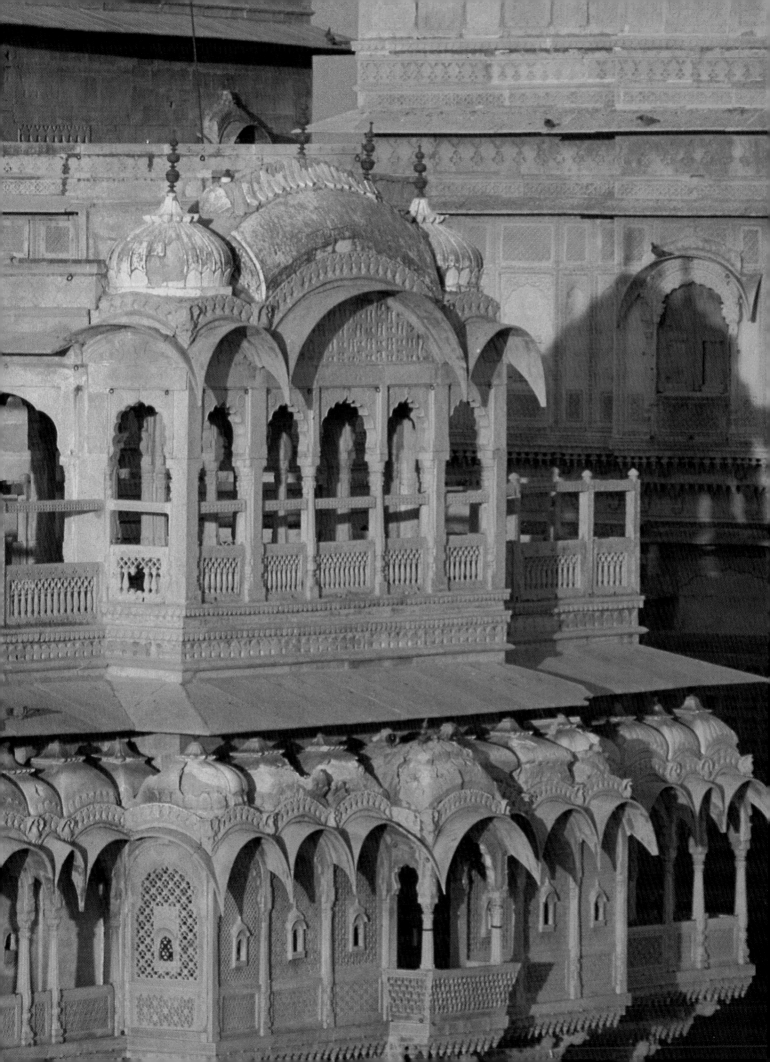

Rajasthan

PAKISTAN

THAR (GREAT INDIAN) DESERT

Bikaner

Mandawa
Dundlod • Nawalgarh
Fatehpur • SHEKHAWATI

Alwar
Bharatpur

Barabagh
Jaisalmer
Lake Gadsisar

Amber
Jaipur ●
Sariska

Osyian
Pushkar
Jodhpur
Ajmer

Aravali Range

Ranthambhore

Bundi ●

Kota ●

Ranakpur

Mount Abu ▲
Udaipur
Lake Pichola
Chittorgarh

New Delhi
Jaipur • Agra

Bombay

INTRODUCTION

THE INDIAN STATE OF RAJASTHAN, just south of Delhi, shares its western border with Pakistan. The state as we know it today, came into being in the wake of Indian independence when 21 princely states of the former Rajputana, and the British enclave of Ajmer-Mewara, were merged. Its area of over 342,000 square kilometres (132,000 square miles) presents intriguing contrasts and immense variety. The Thar Desert stretching to the horizon in all directions, and the Aravali Range with its numerous fortresses on its ridges, are the two prominent features of this land. The Thar Desert extends from the Sahara to the Great Gobi deserts. It moves from west to northeast while the Aravali Hills cut across it from northeast to southwest, dividing the green region on the east from the barren plains of the northwest and west. The colour that nature denied to western Rajasthan has been provided by its bright and lively people.

Fossils dating back 180 million years have been found at Akal near Jaisalmer, but the earliest man-made remains belong mainly to the Indus Valley or Harppan Civilization (2500 BC), though some excavations near Kalibhanga in northern Rajasthan have brought to light traces of a pre-Harppan population as well.

Several references to this region are found in ancient historical documents, but it gained in importance only during the medieval period, with the rise of the Rajput dynasties and the advent of Islam in India. It is from this period that the great tales of romance, pride, valour, chivalry and sacrifice arose. Because of the central role the Rajput principalities played during this period, the region came to be known as *Rajputana* (the abode of princes). Believing themselves to be descendants of the sea, moon and fire, the Rajputs emerged as a prominent martial race. For many years, they relentlessly fought the Mughals in a bid for supremacy and independence. The imposing forts bear silent testimony to their amazing heroism and tenacity. But their prolonged resistance was overwhelmed by the better equipped Mughal forces. The far-sighted Mughals recognized the military skill of the Rajputs, and the subsequent mutual dependence that developed between some major Rajput houses and the Mughal emperors is a striking feature of medieval Indian history.

The decline of the Rajput kingdoms began with the disintegration of the Mughal Empire, and British cunning completed the process. Pretending to protect the Rajputs from the Marathas, then a rising power in Central India, the British persuaded the Rajputs into signing treaties subordinating themselves to the paramount power of the British Crown. British residents were posted in the states to gradually take charge of all major affairs, including matters of succession and matrimonial alliances. It was ironic that the Rajput princes, whose forefathers had fought for centuries in defiance of Mughal rule, meekly accepted British supremacy. In later years, they identified more with the British than their fellow countrymen and the freedom movement in Rajasthan was directed as much against loyalist Indian princes as for independence, the end of princely rule was inevitable.

It was not only in the battlefields that the Rajputs and Mughals interacted as either adversaries or allies, but in the world of art too. The Rajputs were great connoisseurs of painting and, inspired by the Mughal school, they developed their own distinctive styles of miniature painting. They patronized painters, craftsmen and performing artists, and it was their highly developed aesthetic sense that turned Rajasthan into an area of such artistic richness. They built cities, forts, palaces and temples that are amongst the largest and most sumptuous in the world. On hill-tops, deep in forests, in the middle of lakes, everywhere are fairy-tale palaces, each with its history and legends of valour and self-sacrifice, of pomp and gaiety, of love and romance. Some of these palaces are today splendid museums with rich collections; others are lavish hotels preserving the ambience and luxury of princely times. The royal hunting reserves are now national parks and sanctuaries, where the visitor can see spectacular varieties of birds and animals.

The Dargah Sharif at Ajmer is India's most important Muslim shrine (top). Jain temples are a distinctive feature of many towns in Rajasthan (centre). Most of Rajasthan's older towns are entered through elaborately designed gateways (above).

Outside the forts and palaces, in Rajasthan's villages, life is no less colourful, despite the total contrast to wealth and grandeur. The dazzling turbans of the magnificently moustached men, and gay *odhanies* and *ghaghras* of the women brighten the whole countryside. Each face, young or old, is a delightful picture.

Delhi and Bombay lie northeast and south of Rajasthan. A journey can easily be undertaken from north to south or from south to north, covering the major destinations — the capitals of the more prominent of the former princely states, with their forts, palaces and temples. On this route are the celebrated Pink City of Jaipur, the Lake City of Udaipur and the three towns of the Desert Triangle — Jodhpur, Jaisalmer and Bikaner. Most of these major towns are linked by air but, if Rajasthan is to be 'felt' not just 'seen', a journey by road is a better way to travel.

Jaipur is the most frequented city. The reasons, of course, are its fame and its proximity to Delhi. Together with Agra, the city of the Taj Mahal, and Delhi it forms the 'Golden Triangle'. Built in the 18th century, it was perhaps the most well-planned city of its time. It takes its name from its founder-ruler, Jai Singh. An astronomer and a man of gifted vision, Jai Singh decided to shift his capital from nearby Amber and build a new city to meet the requirements of his people. He planned his dream city in collaboration with his architect, Diwan Vidyadhar. A simple grid system was adopted which divided the city into seven rectangular blocks with wide roads and *chaupars* (well-defined squares). In the heart of the city, the Raja built his palace and his famous observatory. Residential areas were earmarked for various communities and groups of craftsmen. Open terraces were provided on either side of the roads so that subjects could watch the royal processions.

The City Palace Museum, the Observatory and Hawa Jahal, meaning the Palace of Winds, along with the forts, palaces and temples of the abandoned capital of Amber, 11 kilometres (7 miles) away, are major places of interest. In the City Palace are two huge silver vessels, recently listed in the *Guinness Book of World Records* as the biggest silver objects in existence.

Next on the track is Udaipur, famous as the city of lakes. There is more to be seen here than in any other region of Rajasthan. Surrounded by three lakes, the city wears a delicate look. The imposing City Palace on the banks of Lake Pichola is the key monument of the town. A boat ride on the serene Pichola lake at sunset affords a most memorable view of its remarkable architecture. Part of the palace today houses a museum displaying the royal collection while another section is the Hotel Shiv Niwas. It is, however, the palace built in the middle of Lake Pichola that has made Udaipur known the world over.

The road westwards leads to Jodhpur, the gateway to the desert. Founded in 1459, the fort of Jodhpur, Mahrangarh, stands majestically on a rock; its towering ramparts, strong bastions and lavishly embellished palaces reflecting the warlike but opulent life-style of the Rajputs. Gilded ceilings and walls are adorned with paintings of the Jodhpur school. A fabulous collection of palanquins, cradles for princes, elephant howdahs, weapons and shields has been laid out.

Another interesting building is Umaid Bhawan Palace built in the 1940s. It is the last of the great palaces in Rajasthan. When seen from a distance, its dome and minarets remind one of the Taj Mahal. The ruins of the former Jodhpur capital and site at Mandore of the cenotaphs of the royal families are also worth visiting. Jaisalmer is a jewel in the desert, and is perhaps the most fascinating fortress in India, for it represents the exquisite artistry of the desert craftsmen. Unlike other forts long abandoned, it still throbs with life, for over 5,000 people still live in the extraordinary network of lanes within its yellow sandstone walls. The detail and precision in the carvings of the *havelies* (mansions) and temples is amazing; the intricately latticed windows and screens in sandstone are more reminiscent of lace. Also around Jaisalmer are scattered the fascinating ruins of the former capital of Lodurya and the abandoned villages of the Paliwal Brahmins.

From Jaisalmer, one moves to Bikaner which was founded by one of the sons of the founder of Jodhpur. Its well-preserved fort, Junagarh, has a rare collection of Sanskrit and Persian manuscripts, miniature paintings of the Bikaner school and weapons. Within the fort the three palaces, Anoop Mahal, Chandra Mahal and Phool Mahal, have fantastic interiors. Floral motifs, delicately inlaid with mirrorwork, cover the ceilings of Phool Mahal; the ceilings of Anoop Mahal reflect the richness of a Persian carpet. The camel-breeding farm near Bikaner offers the visitor an earthy contrast to the magnificence of the palaces.

The temple architecture of Rajasthan is mainly Jain though fine examples of eighth to fifteenth-century Hindu temples are also spread all over Rajasthan. The temples of Jagat, near Udaipur, are said to be the forerunners of the celebrated temples of Khajuraho. The best examples of temple architecture in Rajasthan are to be seen at Mount Abu, its solitary hill-station. The Dilwara temples there are a fantasy in marble. The celebrated flower pendant that hangs from a ceiling and the pillars and arches are all exquisitely carved. Colonel Tod took great pride in claiming Abu as his discovery. He felt that no Gothic building could match the beauty of the temples there. Between Mount Abu and Jodhpur is another group of remarkable Jain temples, those at Ranakpur. Of the 1,444 profusely carved columns to be seen there, not one repeats the same design.

There is much more to be discovered in Rajasthan.

Many of the glorious but less visited forts, like that of Chittorgarh, are not on the main routes. The two regions of Shekhawati and Hadoti unfold a rich heritage of wall-paintings and temples. There are also the three picturesque wildlife sanctuaries. At Ranthambhore and Sariska, there are tigers, leopards, chinkaras, sambhars and blue bulls, and an amazing variety of birds. Bharatpur, one of Asia's most important bird sanctuaries, attracts migratory birds from Siberia and Central Asia from October onwards. The number of species recorded by ornithologists is indeed incredible.

Rajasthan during a fair or a festival is a riot of colour. Full of spirit, the people of Rajasthan love celebrations. It is said that the Rajasthanis celebrate nine festivals a week! Barring the listless summer months, every season here is marked with festivity. In the long list of fairs, the one at Pushkar tops the list. Held on the fullmoon day in the month of Kartik (October–November), the fair draws tens of thousands in their colourful best. Pushkar is a small town 143 kilometres (90 miles) from Jaipur. Its lake is sacred to the Hindus since it is believed that when Lord Brahma, the creator of the universe, killed a demon with a lotus on this spot, its petals struck the earth and water gushed out, forming the lake. Brahma, who was looking for a place to perform a Vedic sacrifice in order to establish his abode on earth, resolved to enact it there, making the spot forever sacred. Brahma's sacrifice was made on the fullmoon day in the month of Kartik, so a dip in the lake on that day each year is believed to be especially auspicious. The only temple in India dedicated to Lord Brahma is located at Pushkar and the worshippers, after taking their dip, gather at the temple to seek his blessings. Both religious devotion and the camel fair draw a huge crowd from the surrounding villages. Pushkar, otherwise a sleepy town, throbs with life during the fair. Merry-go-rounds, street theatre and camel races keep the villagers thoroughly entertained and the event is an unforgettable spectacle.

While there are a number of traditional festivals and fairs, some of them have been revived or created to preserve tradition and attract tourists. When princes still ruled, state festivals full of pomp and pageantry were held. One that has survived with the help of the Rajasthan Department of Tourism, is the Gangaur Festival, which is celebrated in March–April. Each state celebrated the festival in its own way and the state records spelled out the arrangements and procedures for the event. With the incorporation of the states in the Indian Union, the former ruling families have either continued with the tradition on a low-key or have abandoned it altogether. Of the created festivals, the Desert Festival at Jaisalmer has been one of the greatest

A crouching mythical creature in a position of supplication

The range of temple architecture in Rajasthan reflects the many influences on the area in the last thousand years (centre). Birds wing round a tower at sunrise (above).

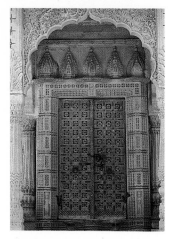

The intricacies of relief work in stone and wood on facades, doors, balconies and windows reveal the Rajasthani love for an almost Gothic profusion of decoration.

Right
This painted door leaf shows Lord Krishna playing his flute.

successes. For three days, in January–February, the region, which is particularly rich in rhythmic tradition, presents local folk-music and dances. On fullmoon day, the festival concludes and the grand finale takes place on the silver sand-dunes.

Music is the core of life in Rajasthan. It is music and song that enable people to face the hardships of life in a severe climate. When in summer the mercury rises over 40°C (104°F) desert dwellers, despite a scorching sun, cheerfully carry on with building roads to the rhythm of community singing. The variety of songs and dances in all of Rajasthan is vast, but it is in the desert region that the musical traditions are richest. Perhaps these people find in music the strength to come to terms with nature's harshness.

The patronage the Langars and the Managaniyars (the two professional entertainer castes) enjoyed over the centuries from the princely families has contributed significantly to Rajasthan's tremendous heritage of rhythmic sounds. The characteristic instruments of these communities are the *satara* (double flute); the two-stringed *sarangi* and *kamaycha*; the *murla-akin* (snake-charmer's flute); the *khartal*, four pieces of wood played like Spanish castanets; the *surnai*, a simple version of the *shehanai*; and the *morchang*, similar to the jew's harp. These professional entertainers sing songs inviting and celebrating the monsoon, carrying lovers' messages and describing the ordeal of a young belle fetching water from a distant pond. Apart from these two communities, there are several other professional entertainers like puppeteers, snake-charmers and acrobats. There are also performers connected with religious ritual. Naths, for example, dance on beds of fire and the Kamads perform *Terhtali*. In this, the dancers will perform with a pot balanced on their heads, and a sword held in their mouths, and will strike a metallic disc tied to their limbs as they dance!

The royal patronage of all manner of craftsmen from far and wide encouraged a thriving and rich tradition of local crafts. These include hand-cut precious and semi-precious stones; jewellery, enamelled and inlaid with precious stones; hand-printed and embroidered textiles and furnishings; miniatures; paintings; carved and enamelled brassware; marble statuary; carpets and rugs; blue pottery and more.

Jaipur is the centre for these crafts; cutting and polishing precious stones, particularly emeralds, is the main industry of this town. Jaipur gems have found their way to the international market and account for a trade involving millions of dollars. Hand-printed and embroidered textiles are other important export items. Traditional and tribal silver jewellery cater for the ethnic taste. But buying these art objects is an art in itself and distinguishing the original from the copy requires knowledge and skill. In Rajasthan, tourists can live like maharajas, for a price. The palace hotels give a taste of the luxurious life of the privileged of yesteryears. After the feudal system was dissolved, many rulers entered the hotel business, foreseeing the growth of the tourism industry. They turned their huge palaces into luxurious hotels in a bid to retain the splendour of those buildings as well as earn good money. The palace hotels of Rajasthan have proved to be a great attraction. Two of them, the Rambagh Palace of Jaipur and the Lake Palace of Udaipur have figured in lists of the best hotels of the world. A number of other palaces and hunting resorts are being converted into hotels. Other members of former royal families have turned their lavish residences into legendary resorts which are different from the palace hotels. They are smaller, less expensive and generally managed by the families themselves.

For budget tourists, a well-spread network of tourist bungalows is provided by the Rajasthan government-supported agency, the Rajasthan Tourism Development Corporation.

Rajasthan is perhaps India's most joyous, glittering and enchanting region; it leaves the visitor with memories of citadels and palaces, lakes and deserts, rhythms, smells and tastes, and a desire to one day return to witness again its exotic cities and people.

Status and community are revealed by various head wear worn.

The brightly coloured costumes and exquisite jewellery add colour to an otherwise barren landscape.

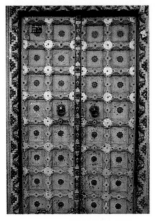

Above
The Jal Mahal, a few miles north of Jaipur, is one of many pleasure palaces and pavilions built by Rajput princes and rulers throughout Rajasthan. Here the Aravali Range encloses a lake famous for migratory duck that winter in the area.

Top
The peacock has inspired artists and poets throughout history. The design above a gateway off the Pritam Niwas Chowk in front of the Chandra Mahal in Jaipur's City Palace has given its name to the wrongly known 'peacock doorway'.

Left
Several of the doors in the City Palace are decorated with finely worked brass panels placed over wooden frames.

Below
Nakkar Darwaza is one of many entrances to Jai Singh II's magnificent City Palace.

Above
One of the remarkable aspects of Diwan Vidyadhar's design for Jai Singh's city is the incorporation of wide streets and squares, locally known as chaupars, *which handle even today's traffic.*

Above right
The Hawa Mahal, or Wind Palace on the east wall of the City Palace compound was added by Sawai Pratap Singh in 1799. Used originally as a gallery for the women of the Zennana to watch processions and parades through the city street, the Hawa Mahal today houses a small museum.

Right
The facade of the Hawa Mahal is remarkable for its perfect symmetry of brick and latticework.

Far left and right
The bazaar around Hawa Mahal and Bari Chaupar, known for local crafts and artefacts, is as popular with locals as it is with visitors.

Above
Amber, 12 kilometres (eight miles) north of Jaipur, was the former capital of the Kachawa rulers before Jai Singh shifted to his new city. Ruins of the older part of Amber date back to the 11th century. The great fort-palace, built during the 16th and 17th centuries still stands.

Left
The surrounding hills are ringed with fortifications, watch-towers and defence walls. Above the Amber Fort, the Jaigarh Fort houses the treasury.

Below
Within the Amber Fort a series of palace buildings, courtyards and a temple were built by successive rulers. The Ganesh Pol leads from the Diwan-I-Am (Hall of Public Audience) area to the Jai Mandir (Diwan-I-Khas), known for its beautiful inlaid mirrorwork.

Left
During the Pushkar Fair, after taking a dip in the holy lake on the day of Kartik Purnima (full moon), the villagers throng to the Brahma Temple. It is believed that the Pushkar Lake was formed when Brahma, the creator of the universe, killed a demon with a lotus during his search for a place to perform a sacrifice. The lake was formed where the lotus fell. It is reputed to be the only temple dedicated to Brahma which is used for worship.

Right
A woman returns from a morning's foraging with a sizeable bundle of sticks. Wood and cow dung are the two major sources of fuel in Rajasthan, although deforestation exacerbates the already desert-like conditions.

There are several animal fairs in Rajasthan but because of its association with a religious event the Pushkar Mela is important. Camels are brought from throughout the state, and along with horses, are traded over a period of ten days. The camel is an essential part of Rajasthani village life. It is a reliable beast of burden, a form of transport in an inhospitable terrain and a provider of wool and milk, and dung for fuel.

There are a tremendous variety of people and colours at the fair. Small stalls trade in camel decorations, saddles, swords, knives, shoes and bags made with camel leather, silver jewellery and blankets. In recent years, Pushkar Mela has developed into a major international attraction.

In the evenings, folk performers sing,
dance and entertain at Rajasthan
Tourism's camp.

Above
Colourful Kanjar dancers from the Kota
region give a vibrant performance.

Left
A young boy from the Bhopa community
playing the traditional string instrument
known as ravanhatta. Bhopas continue the
great oral tradition, recounting stories of
Rajasthan's folk heroes, such as Pabuji,
Dev Narayan and Ramdeo.

Right
The community of snake charmers known
as Kalbelias are also skilled dancers and
singers.

Ajmer, 13 kilometres (eight miles) west of Pushkar and 130 kilometres (81 miles) south of Jaipur, is the major Muslim centre in Rajasthan. Around 1191, a Persian called Khwaja Muinuddin Chishti moved to Ajmer from Mecca and established the Chishtiya sect of the Sufi order. After his death in 1236, his tomb, Dargarh Sharif, became the most important Muslim shrine in South Asia. Each year, death anniversary celebrations or urs draw tens of thousands of pilgrims to the tomb.

Apart from Ajmer, most of the major towns in Rajasthan have substantial Muslim communities who play a significant role in maintaining traditional performing arts and many crafts.

The small princely town of Bundi was the capital of the senior state in the Hadoti region of southeastern Rajasthan. In art circles, Bundi is famous for its 18th-century miniature paintings. The panels on the walls of the Chitra Shala in the Bundi Palace show the love legends of Krishna and the romance of royal life. Rudyard Kipling witnessed some of the most recent murals being painted when he visited Bundi in 1887.

Above
Kota's small Jagmandir Palace on an island in Lake Kishor Sagar, was built around 1740 by Maharani Brij Kunwar.

Left
The Kota school of painting, though distinct from that of Bundi, incorporates many similar themes. Here a wall painting shows the Kota family deity, Shri Brijnathji Maharaj, in a ceremonial procession.

Above
Among the subjects common to Rajasthan's various schools of miniature and wall painting are the legends and exploits of Lord Krishna.

Right
The arid landscape of Rajasthan is enlivened by villagers' use of bright colours in turbans, saris or animal decorations. Here India's national colours have been painted on a bull's horns.

39

Top
*The huge fort of Chittorgarh,
covering over 270 hectares (700
acres), 116 kilometres (72 miles)
east of Udaipur, is a symbol of
valour and patriotism. Until
1567, the fort was among the
most fiercely contested seats of
power in western India.*

Above left and right
*Elephants feature in both the
mundane and supramundane.
Two elephants depicted in
battle, while Ganesh — the
elephant god — clasps his
consorts.*

Right
*The 36-metre (120-foot) -high
Vijay Stambh was erected to
celebrate Rana Kumbha's
defeat of neighbouring Muslim
rulers.*

Overlooking Udaipur's Pichola lake, the
imposing City Palace is, in fact, a series of
different palaces built by successive rulers
of Mewar (above). The main buildings form
a large museum while the most recently
built palace has been converted into
Rajasthan's most luxurious hotel, The
Hotel Shiv Niwas. Some of the palace
buildings have ornate mirrorwork (right)
and miniature paintings. Many of the glass
inlay figures are portraits of historical
figures (centre).

Top
Jag Niwas is one of two island palaces in Lake Pichola. It was one of the first to be converted to a hotel. The Lake Palace Hotel is considered one of the world's best, and certainly one of the most romantic.

43

Left
Mount Abu, on Rajasthan's southern border with Gujarat, is the highest point in the Aravali Range that runs through the state. The Dilwara temples, north of the town, are exquisitely carved Jain temples. Built in white marble, the temples date back to the 11th and 13th centuries. Many of the carvings on ceilings, pillars and torans (arches) depict aspects of Jain philosophy.

Right
The temples at Ranakpur set among forested hills between Udaipur and Jodhpur are fine examples of Jain architecture. The main Chaumucha Temple, dedicated to Lord Adinath, covers a large area and needs 1,444 intricately carved pillars, of which no two are the same, to support the roof.

Left
Jodhpur's Umaid Bhawan was the last great palace to be built in India. Started in 1929 as a famine relief project, employing up to 3,000 people each day, the palace took 16 years to complete. Part of it is now a museum, part of it is a hotel and one wing is still home to the royal family of Jodhpur.

Above
Jaswant Thada was built in 1899 as a cenotaph for Jaswant Singh of Jodhpur, beside the road leading down from the fort. The cenotaph of marble from the Makrana mines was the first to be built away from Mandore.

The majestic Mahrangarh Fort dominates the town of Jodhpur below it. Within the strong walls of the fort are the fine palaces of successive generations of rulers who lived here until the completion of the Umaid Bhawan Palace. The museum, containing the fabulous royal collection, is among the best maintained and planned displays in Rajasthan.

Eight kilometres (five miles) from Jodhpur, is the former capital of its Rathore rulers. Mandore is renowned for its elegant chatris (cenotaphs) of past rulers. Set in well-maintained gardens, the chatris reflect a mixture of styles that became increasingly elaborate as the fortune of the Marwar State increased.

During the reign of Ajit and Abai Singh, in the early 18th century, the rock face opposite the Mandore chatris was carved into a series of statues. The figures are of local Rajput and Hindu deities, including Pabuji, whose legends are recounted by the Bhopas.

The 16 temples in the small village of Osyian, 64 kilometres (40 miles) north of Jodhpur, were built between the eighth and 12th centuries. Earlier temples follow orthodox Hindu styles; later ones were built by Jains. The largest temple is dedicated to Lord Mahavir, the founder of the Jain faith. The 12th-century Sachiya Mata Temple is the most important piece of architecture.

Village wells, tanks and ponds are still the main source of water in most areas of the state. They are carefully preserved in areas where the monsoon comes every third year.

Women who collect and carry water are known as paniharnis *and many folk songs celebrate their poise and beauty. Some songs refer to the creation of ponds and wells by a paniharni's lover, the difficulties of the work, the tearing of a veil or pursuit by an admirer.*

The traffic police have a never-ending struggle maintaining control and discipline on Rajasthan's roads. The problems of resting cattle, slow bullock carts, tongas, the occasional elephant, camels and fast cars are confused by bicycles and scooters weaving their way through the chaos; visitors are frequently left bemused, anxious, but often entertained.

The Thar, or Great Indian Desert, stretches along Rajasthan's western border with Pakistan. Rising out of the desert is the city of Jaisalmer, built on a triple-peaked rock known as Trikuta in 1156. At the base of the hill, the man-made Lake Gadsisar was the only source of water for the town. Many of the surrounding buildings and steps were built by Telia, a well-known courtesan.

Above
*The royal chatris of the former rulers, at
Barabagh, a few kilometres outside
Jaisalmer. Each canopied and pillared
chatri marks the site of a ruler's
cremation. The view of the city from
Barabagh at sunset is spectacular.*

Right
*Before building the city of Jaisalmer, the
Bhati rulers' capital was at Lodurya, 16
kilometres (ten miles) to the northeast.
The Jain temple is still a popular place of
pilgrimage.*

In Jaisalmer the exteriors of most buildings are decorated. The fine carving, latticework and rare inlay work in the yellow sandstone on the facades of homes has given the city its reputation as a living museum.

Above and right
The early 19th-century Patwon Haveli took 50 years to complete and is perhaps the best known of Jaisalmer's many wonderful buildings. Two other important havelis, Nathmalji Ki and Salim Singh were built by, and named after, prime ministers.

Left
The simple and traditional mud buildings of the neighbouring villages are effective against the harsh desert climate.

Aspects of daily life reflect the gentle flow of Rajasthan; a pipe smoker inhales his mixture; street musicians tinkle away; a tailor rests in his doorway; and street murals expound the wisdom of Gandhi, and the beauty of hand-hennaring.

The third great city of the desert is
Bikaner, which recently celebrated its
500th year of independence from Jodhpur.
The squat domes of the Bhandeshwar
Temple (left) stand over its pillared
entrance, and emphasize the elegantly
carved tower behind. Inside the cool halls
of this and other temples and palaces,
marble friezes (above) portray historical
and religious events that often reflect the
wealth and prestige of local rulers.

Lelgarh Palace was designed at the turn of the century by Sir Swinton Jacob for, perhaps the greatest modern Indian ruler, Maharaja Ganga Singh. The palace is built in a soft-red sandstone from nearby quarries and finely carved by local craftsmen. Part of it has been converted into a museum, part into a private hotel and the remaining portion houses the descendants of Ganga Singh.

The region of Shekhawati, in northwestern Rajasthan, has recently become known for the extraordinary wall paintings and frescoes both in and outside many of the havelis. The influences on the artist were not the Indian seasons, poetry or music but rather pictures and reports from a newly industrialized world. Trains, early cars, gramaphones, telephones and even a portrait of Queen Victoria reveal the European influence. Towns of the region, such as Mandawa, Dundlod, Fatehpur, Ramgarh and Nawalgarh have the finest examples of the paintings.

The architecture around the tank next to the City Palace in Alwar emphasizes the importance given to conserving any source of water.

Water washed over the small footprints at the Moosi Maharani Chatri near the tank and collected, is reputed to have medicinal properties suited to children. The chatri is one of the best preserved of its type and the fading gold-leaf painting within the dome depicts various mythological themes.

The villagers who flock to fairs and melas, such as Pushkar, are one of the great attractions of Rajasthan. Posing on props, such as a motorbike or behind the wheel of a cardboard car, the villagers take home souvenir photographs that make the occasion one to remember.

Following pages
The fierce heat of the day subsides as the sun sets and cooling winds bring relief.